DRAW SUPER MANGA! MONSTERS

DAVID OKUM

IMPACT
CINCINNATI, OHIO
www.impact-books.com

How to Use This Book

There are three or four steps for each monster.

Trace over step 1.

Lay your traced paper over step 2 and add the missing lines.

For step 3, add the details you see and erase the extra lines.

Darken the important lines on the last step and you're finished!

Shapes

Everything is made up of shapes: circles, squares, rectangles and triangles.

Copy or trace some of these shapes. If you can draw these, you can draw anything!

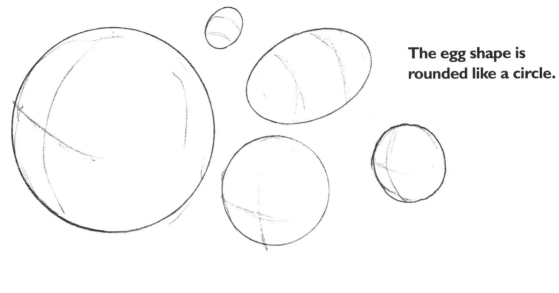

The egg shape is rounded like a circle.

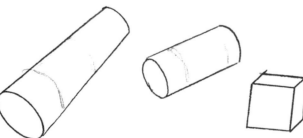

How many squares can you find in this cube?

The ends of these cylinders are circles.

See the triangles in this spaceship?

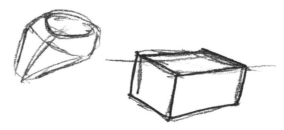

Monster Legs

Animal vs. Human Legs

Some monsters have animal-like back legs. This means that their weight rests on the balls of the feet and the ankle acts as a backwards knee.

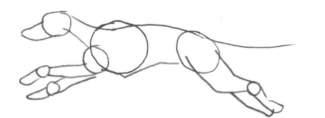

The Four-Legged Run

Animals or monsters with four legs, called *quadrupeds,* use their front legs to pull forward and their back legs to push forward. That's how they run so fast.

Wings

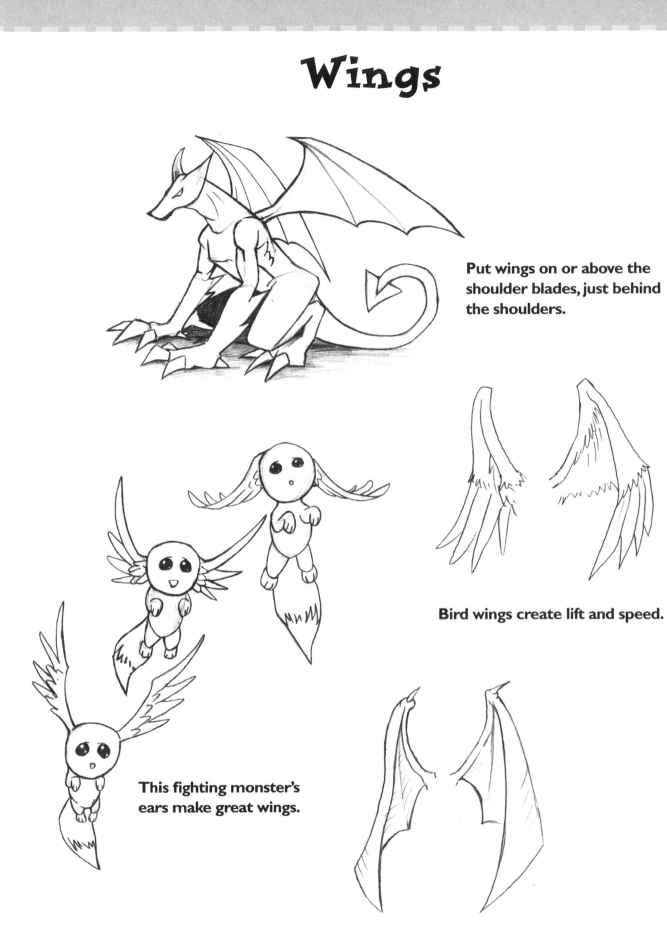

Put wings on or above the shoulder blades, just behind the shoulders.

Bird wings create lift and speed.

This fighting monster's ears make great wings.

The bat-like wings allow dragons to make fast turns.

Fur and Claws

Monster Fur

Fur makes a huge impact on his looks. Short hair looks totally different from long hair.

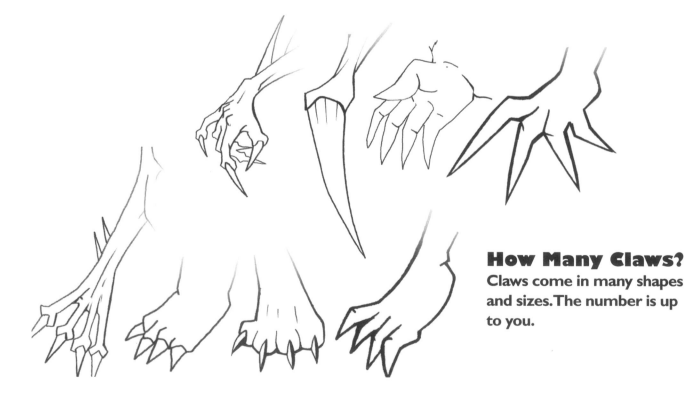

How Many Claws?

Claws come in many shapes and sizes. The number is up to you.

Tails and Fangs

Many monsters use their tails for balance or to move. Devils and demons usually have arrow-point tails. Lizards and dinosaurs have spiny tails.

Meat eaters need sharp, pointy teeth and plant eaters have flat teeth. Beaks do not have teeth, but giving a beak teeth makes any monster look scary.

Mini-Dragon

Cabbit Mascot

4

MONSTER PETS
Robot Mascot

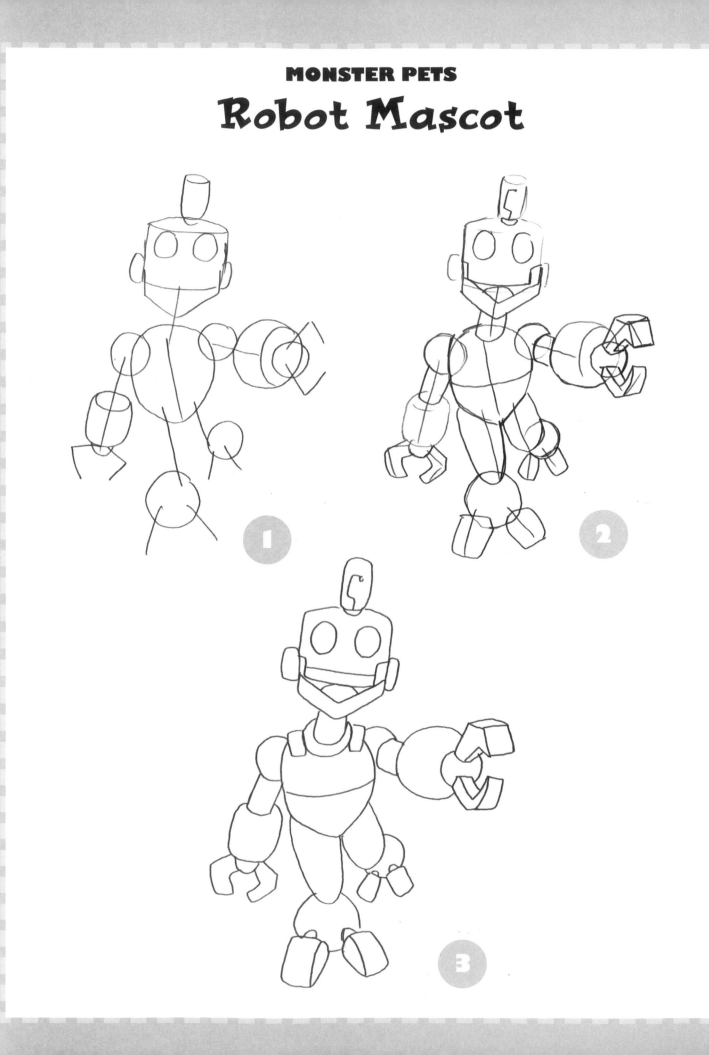

MONSTER PETS
Monkey Fighter

Little Sprites

Orb Critter

Snow Beastie

Elemental Creatures

Tyrannosaur

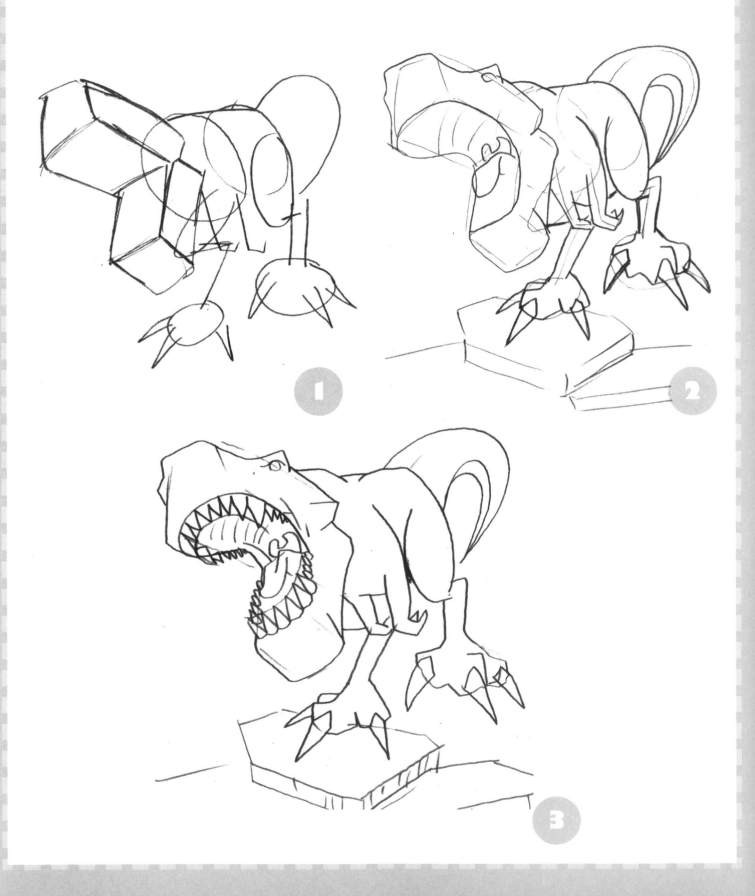

4

GIANT MONSTERS
Triceratops

Giant Lizard

4

GIANT MONSTERS
Giant Ape

GIANT MONSTERS
Giant Robot

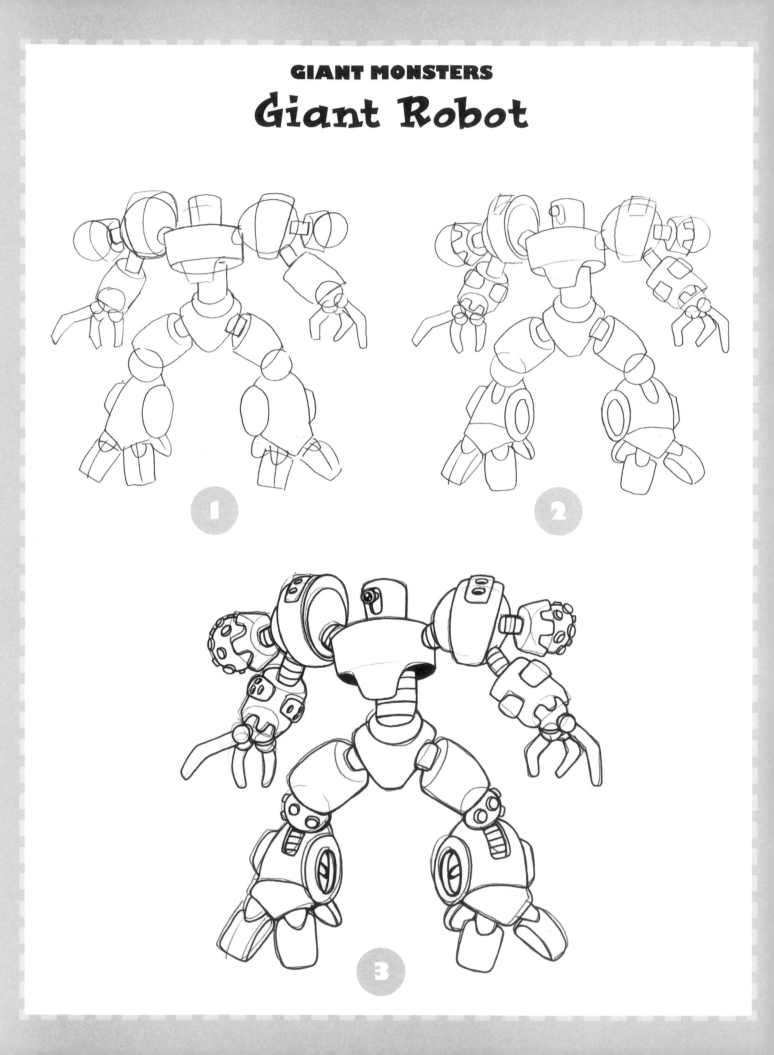

4

Sea Serpent

Giant Insect

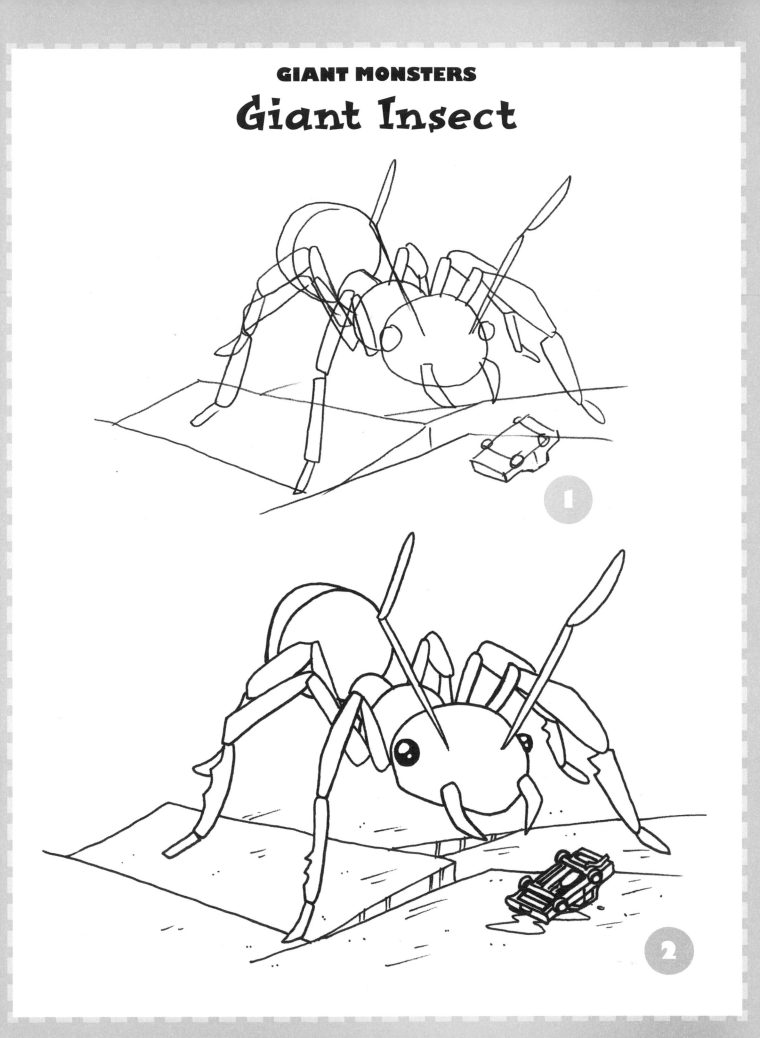

Psychic Warrior

MUTANTS
Cat Warrior

4

MUTANTS
Beastman

Bat-Winged Warrior

Sea Creature

Metal Man

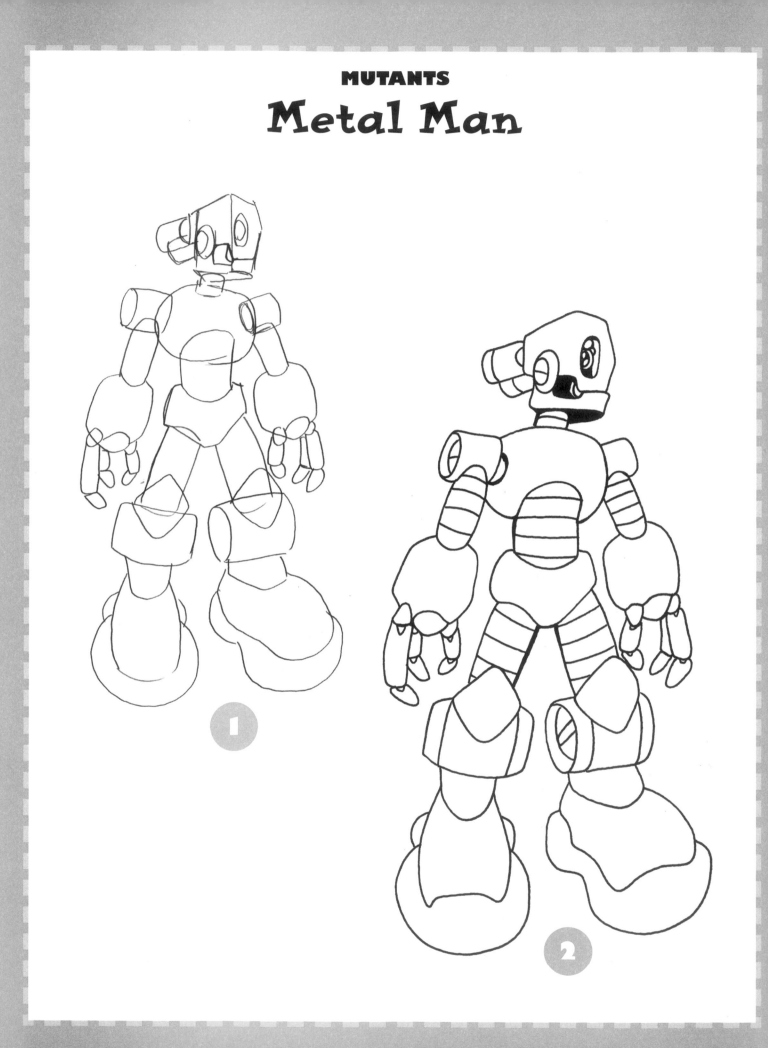

Merfolk

MUTANTS

Mutant Thug

Mutant Cyborg

ALIENS
Invader Leader

4

ALIENS
Invader Beast

Alien Monster

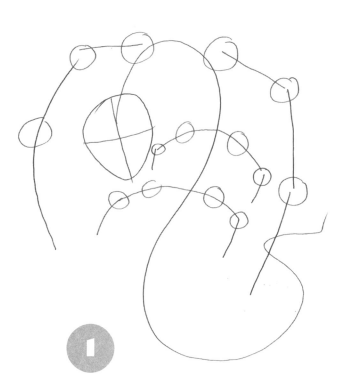

1

2

3

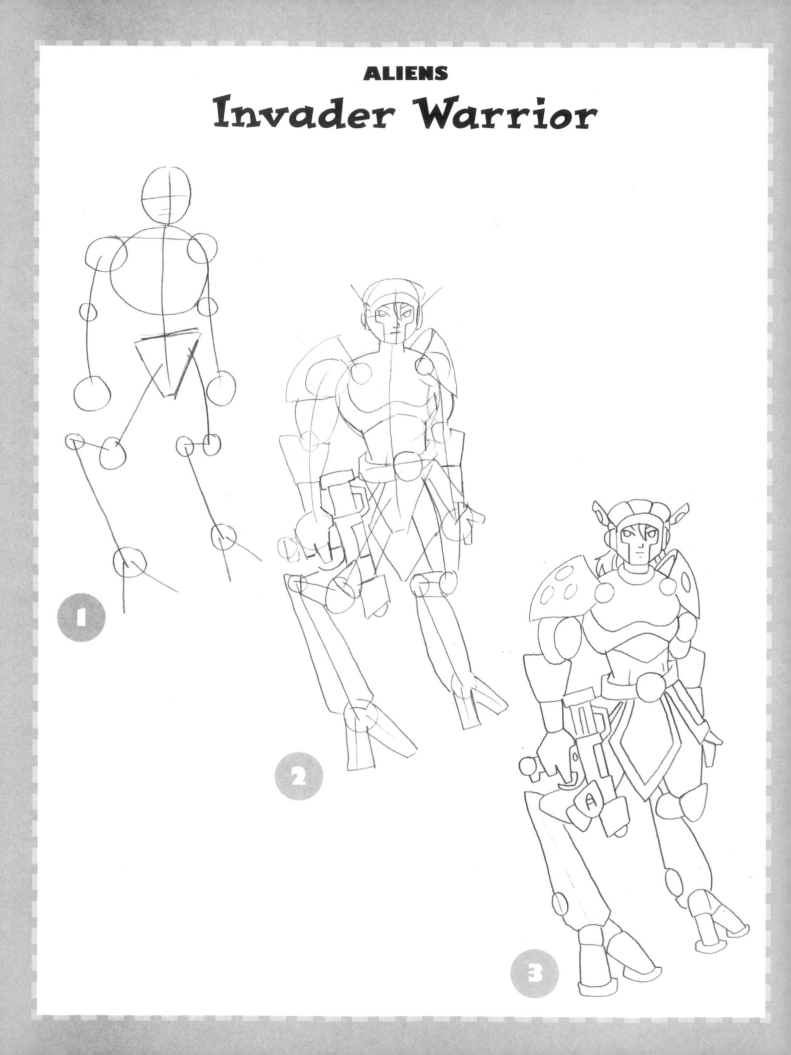

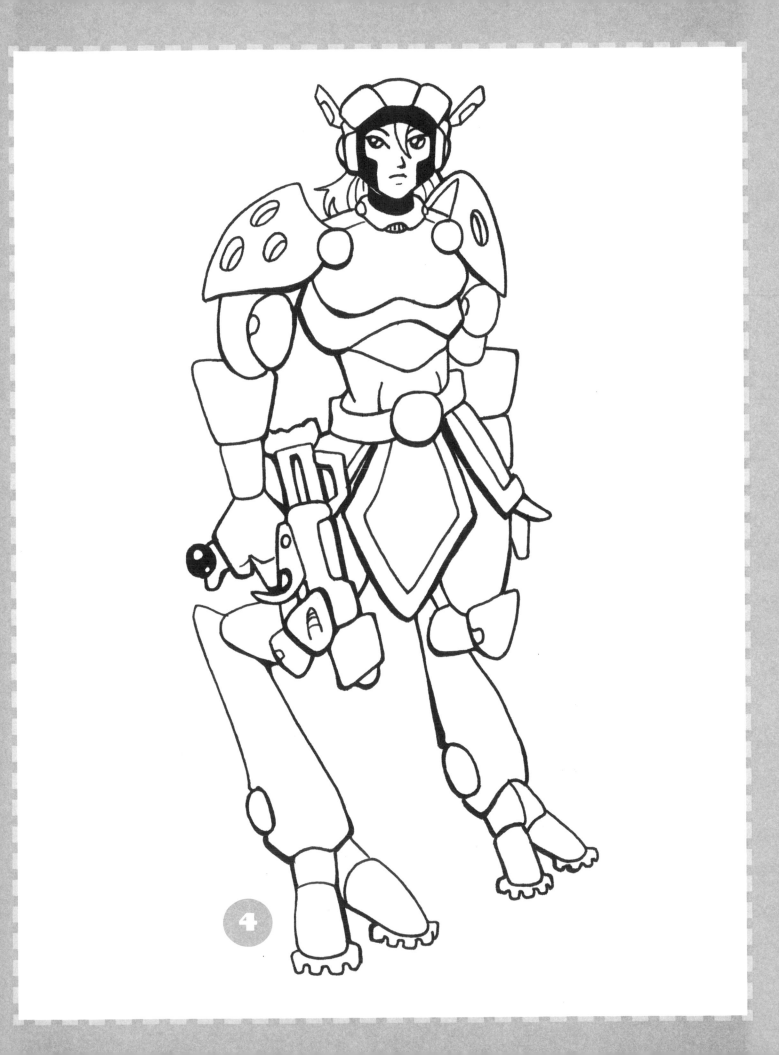

Alien Pet

ALIENS
Cosmic Warlord

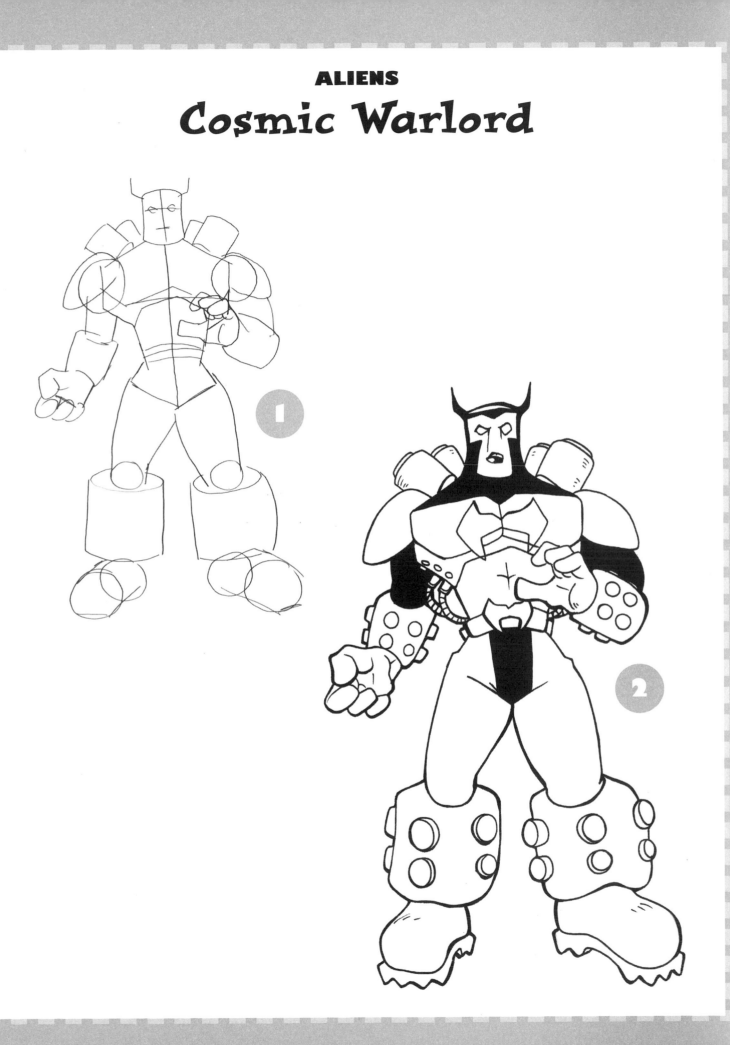

Dragon

4

FANTASY
Ogre

FANTASY
Unicorn

FANTASY
Gargoyle

About the Author

David Okum has worked as a freelance artist and illustrator since 1984 and has had his manga work published since 1992, beginning with a story in a Ninja High School anthology published by Antarctic Press. He has since been included in two other Antarctic Press anthologies and several small-press comic books. His writing and artwork have appeared in six books by Guardians of Order, publishers of Big Eyes, Small Mouth (the anime and manga role-playing game).

David studied fine art and history at the University of Waterloo and works as a high school art teacher.

Other fine Impact books are available from your local bookstore, art supply store or direct from the publisher.

09 08 07 06 05   5 4 3 2 1

DISTRIBUTED IN CANADA BY FRASER DIRECT
100 Armstrong Avenue
Georgetown, ON, Canada L7G 5S4
Tel: (905) 877-4411

DISTRIBUTED IN THE U.K. AND EUROPE BY DAVID & CHARLES
Brunel House, Newton Abbot, Devon, TQ12 4PU, England
Tel: (+44) 1626 323200, Fax: (+44) 1626 323319
Email: mail@davidandcharles.co.uk

DISTRIBUTED IN AUSTRALIA BY CAPRICORN LINK
P.O. Box 704, S. Windsor NSW, 2756 Australia
Tel: (02) 4577-3555

Library of Congress Cataloging in Publication Data

Okum, David, 1967-
    Draw super manga monsters! / David Okum.— 1st ed.
        p. cm
    ISBN 1-58180-733-3 (pbk. : alk. paper)
    1. Monsters in art--Juvenile literature. 2. Comic books, strips, etc.--Japan--Technique--Juvenile literature. 3. Cartooning--Technique--Juvenile literature. I. Title.
NC1764 .8 . M650575 2005
741.5'0952--dc22   2005006209

Editor: Mona Michael
Production editor: Jenny Ziegler
Designer: Wendy Dunning
Production artist: Brian Schroeder
Production coordinator: Mark Griffin